D-DAY
The Invasion in Photographs

D-DAY

The Invasion in Photographs

Edited by Tony Hall

LONGMEADOW
PRESS

A SALAMANDER BOOK

Prelim captions: Half-title: Speeding
across the Channel, the destroyer HMS
Kelvin takes Winston Churchill to see
the progress of the invasion. Title:
Unloading from an LST, a Crusader
Ack Ack tank of the British 7th
Armoured Division arrives on *Gold*
Beach. Credits: Casualties from *Sword*
Beach are taken aboard the cruiser
HMS *Frobisher*. Contents: An
abandoned Stuart light tank.

CREDITS

Designer: Paul Johnson

Text: Tony Hall

Filmsetting: SX Composing,
  Rayleigh, Essex

Color and mono reproduction:
  P & W Graphics PTE, Singapore

Printed in Belgium by Proost
  International Book Production

PICTURE CREDITS

Front cover: US National Archives,
Washington DC, (USNA); Back cover,
top: National Archives of Canada
(NAC); middle, USNA; bottom: Imperial
War Museum, London (IWM). Page 1:
IWM; 2-3: IWM; 4, 5: IWM; 6-7: IWM;
8-9: All, USNA; 10: Far left, Eisenhower
Library, Abilene, Kansas; Far left,
below, Royal Marines Museum,
Portsmouth; 11: Left, The Tank Museum,
Bovington; Below, NAC; 12: Above,
USNA; Right, Portsmouth City Council;
13: Left, Royal Marines Museum; Below,
IWM; 14: Above, USNA; Right, IWM; 15:
Right, IWM; Below, USNA; 16-17: IWM;
18: Above, IWM; Below, Salamander
Books; 19: Above, USNA; Left, IWM; 20:
Left, IWM; Below left, USNA; 21: Right,
Royal Marines Museum; Below right,
IWM; 22: Above left, USNA; Left,
Airborne Forces Museum, Aldershot;
23: Main photo, USNA; Left, Airborne
Forces Museum; 24-25: USNA; 26-27:
All, USNA; 28-29: All, USNA; 30-31: All,
USNA; 32-33: USNA; 34-35: All, USNA;
36-37: All, USNA; 38-39: All, USNA;
40-41: IWM; 42: Right, Eisenhower
Library; Below, IWM; 43: USNA; 44-45:
All, IWM; 46: Right, Bundesarchiv,
Koblenz, Germany (BUND); Below,
IWM; 47: Left, BUND; Below, IWM;
48-49: IWM; 50: Above, NAC; Right,
IWM; 51: Below, NAC; 52: Left, IWM;
Below, NAC; 53: Left, Royal Marines
Museum; Below, IWM; 54-55: IWM; 56:
Above, IWM; Right, The Tank Museum;
57: Left, The Tank Museum; Below,
Royal Marines Museum; 58: Right,
Airborne Forces Museum; Below, IWM;
59: Both, Airborne Forces Museum;
60-61: All, BUND; 62: Above, Royal
Marines Museum; Below, IWM; 63:
Both, IWM; 64: NAC.

Contents

Publisher's Notes: All times given are
on the 24-hour clock. Operations on
D-Day were timed to double British
Summer time: GMT plus two hours.

Chapter 1

MEN AND ARMIES

The planning of the long-awaited invasion of Europe had been going on since 1943, and by May 1944 enough men and equipment had been assembled in southern England to transform the whole region into one vast armed camp. Here in a quiet street in the south coast port city of Southampton, an American motorized unit awaits the order for embarkation.

Left: In December 1943, General Dwight D. Eisenhower, US Army, was appointed commander of the Allied invasion of Europe, codenamed Operation *Overlord*. General Eisenhower arrived in England on January 15, 1944 to assemble his joint Allied command, known as SHAEF – Supreme Headquarters, Allied Expeditionary Force.

Right and below right: Since 1942 American troops and equipment had been arriving in England in preparation for an invasion. Because of the threat of German U-Boat attacks in the Atlantic this build-up had been slow, but by the beginning of 1944 thousands of troops were being shipped over in merchant ships and converted passenger liners, bringing the total number in Britain by May 1944 to over 1.5 million.

Below: To support the Allied effort, over 5 million tonnes of arms and supplies had been shipped. These are Sherman tanks of a British Army unit.

To help get the troops ashore in France and keep them supplied against German opposition, a whole host of ingenious devices were developed and built in Britain.

Far left: Foremost amongst these were two complete prefabricated harbours – codenamed *Mulberry* – part of which can be seen here in construction. The harbours were to be towed to France a day after D-Day.

Far left, below: At the opposite end of the scale were these folding bicycles being used by British commandos.

A whole range of special tanks, given the name of 'Funnies', were developed to break through German defences. Left: An 'ARK' ramp carrier used by vehicles to get over obstacles. Below: A 'CRAB' flail tank used to destroy mines. (See also pages 56–57.)

The importance of getting men and materiel onto the landing beaches also led to the development of a whole host of special landing craft and ships.

Above: A Landing Ship, Tank (LST), its bow doors allowing the loading of up to 25 motor vehicles or tanks.

Right: A Landing Craft, Tank (LCT), capable of carrying three tanks or 250 tonnes of cargo. (This particular Royal Navy LCT carried American troops on to *Omaha* beach on D-Day.)

Left: To counter the threat of an air attack on the invasion fleet, this Landing Craft, Flak (LCF) carried four two-pounder and eight 20mm anti-aircraft guns.

Below: This Royal Navy crew stand aboard their survey vessel. Small craft such as this made vital reconnaissance trips to France in the weeks prior to D-Day, checking both sea currents and beach conditions. Of the many millions of servicemen about to take part in the invasion, these men already knew where *Overlord* was headed.

Everywhere, the training and preparation for the invasion continued.

Above: US Army infantrymen practise attacks on beach defences in their training area on Slapton Sands on the south Devon coast.

Right: Members of the British Army Royal Signal Corps get their first look at French invasion currency. Printed in the United States and shipped over in their millions, these franc notes, which came in a number of denominations, were paid to Allied service personnel when serving in France.

Right: Both men and equipment had to be in perfect condition for the coming battles. Here a tank crew of the British 13th/18th Hussars clean weapons on top of their Stuart Mk1 light tank – a reconnaissance vehicle, and the most widely used light tank of the war.

Below: A great deal of the soldiers' training revolved around embarking and disembarking from landing craft and ships. It was a task which had to be done in a swift and orderly fashion but which was made no easier by troops weighed down by full assault kit. These heavily laden American infantrymen can be seen training somewhere on the south coast waiting to board a number of Landing Craft, Assault (LCAs).

Chapter 2

THE ARMADA
SAILS

Sub Lieutenant A. Mitchell of the anti-aircraft auxiliary HMS *Aristocrat* pipes his vessel away from its moorings towards the distant coast of France. The order to sail had finally been given. Years of waiting, planning and preparation had come to an end. The biggest amphibious assault in history was underway.

Above: To Allied seamen, like these Royal Navy Warrant Officers, confirmation of the invasion came on April 10, 1944 when orders for the transport of the invasion force codenamed *Neptune* were issued by the Allied Naval Commander-in-Chief Admiral Sir Bertram Ramsay RN. The orders at last revealed the invasion's destination – the Normandy coast, and went on to detail the assault beaches: *Utah* and *Omaha* for the Americans, *Gold, Juno* and *Sword* for the British and Canadians. The landing forces would be designated 21st Army Group and would comprise the US 1st Army and British 2nd Army. In overall command of all these ground troops would be General Sir Bernard Montgomery.

Right: On May 28 General Eisenhower's planned date for the start of the invasion – *Overlord*'s 'D-Day' in military jargon – was announced; it was to be June 5. By May 31 troops such as these US Army infantrymen had begun to file onto their allotted ships and landing craft.

Above: All along the southern coast, in ports and harbours such as this one in Brixham in Devon, loading went on in earnest. But by June 3, the weather had begun to worsen in the English Channel.

Left: In the early hours of June 4 the invasion fleet had begun to sail, but within hours it was recalled – the weather had worsened and the invasion was postponed for 24 hours. The assault troops who had been kept in their transports for up to five days already, would have to wait a little longer.

Because of the changes in the tides, the invasion could not be postponed for long. Timing was becoming critical. In the early hours of June 5, SHAEF's chief meteorological officer presented a forecast promising better weather on June 6. On the strength of this, General Eisenhower gave the order for the invasion to begin.

Left: Convoys of ships and landing craft, such as these Landing Craft, Infantry (LCI), were soon underway. In total the fleet was made up of five separate Task Forces, one for each beach. Each Task Force consisted of between 9 and 16 separate convoys. The combined invasion fleet which set out on June 5 numbered over 5,300 ships and landing craft.

Below left: To defend the landing craft against German attack and to provide a naval bombardment on the assault beaches, the fleet consisted of some 325 warships, including 101 destroyers such as the USS *Thomson* seen here being refuelled. The *Thomson* provided fire-support to the American forces on *Omaha*. Though the fleet consisted mainly of Royal Navy and US Navy ships, it also contained warships from France, Poland, Norway, Greece and The Netherlands.

Right: Throughout the fleet, assault troops such as these Royal Marines received their final briefings. For many it would be the first time they would learn of their destination. Even their training maps in England had been disguised with bogus names to hide the invasion's true target.

Below right: As the fleet sailed on, heralded by minesweepers and protected overhead by Allied aircraft, a whole series of deception plans were being put into operation. Ranging from radar jamming to the dropping of dummy paratroopers, they were carefully designed to hide the movement of the fleet and to fool the Germans as to the invasion's real target. Meanwhile back in England, the airborne forces were about to begin their own dangerous missions.

Above and above left: The American airborne attack would be made on the western flank of the invasion area, behind *Utah* beach. Two divisions, the 101st and 82nd Airborne, in total 13,000 men, would land before dawn to secure the exits from the beach and the beachhead's right flank. Both paratroopers, such as the soldier on the left and glider-borne troops of the 82nd (above), began their long flights to Normandy in the early hours of June 6.

Far left and left: The British airborne assault would be made by the British 6th Airborne Division, which was to land on the eastern flank of the invasion beachhead to the east of *Sword* beach. Its task was to secure the flank and crossings over the vital Orne River and Caen Canal. Like the American force, the British airborne command consisted of paratroopers such as these men emplaning on the far left, and glider-borne troops who were carried into battle in wooden gliders such as the one taking off on the left, which carried 6th Airborne's commander Major General Richard Gale. Note the glider's distinctive black and white 'invasion stripe' identification markings painted on all Allied aircraft used on D-Day.

Chapter 3

UTAH BEACH

Utah was the first assault area in the American sector and formed the right flank of the invasion area which swept on east along the coastline of the Bay of Seine.

The first wave of troops on *Utah* comprised the 8th, 22nd, and 12th Infantry Regiments of the US 4th Infantry Division, US VII Corps commanded by Major General J. Lawton Collins, the first assault corps of Lieutenant General Omar C. Bradley's US 1st Army. Their time for landing was 06:30.

Right: American troops struggle ashore from their landing craft onto *Utah* beach. Note on the left some of the thousands of beach obstacles installed along the coast by the German defenders. (See also page 42).

Right: An Allied minesweeper detects and destroys a German mine off *Utah*. The minesweepers began clearing the approaches to *Utah* at 02:00, June 6, two hours before the arrival of the fleet and over four hours before the assault was due to go in. In all, 97 minesweepers were in operation on D-Day.

Below: A US Coast Guard cutter moors alongside a Landing Craft, Vehicle (LCV) on its way into the beach. The cutters were used as rescue launches during the landing operations.

Above: A mortar team prepares to go into action in the dunes immediately behind *Utah*. The initial waves of troops onto the beach had found it lightly defended. Luckily they had drifted on strong sea currents 2,000 yards (1,800m) south of their allotted sector. Realizing the opportunity, rapid advances were made inland to seize the four vital beach exits and to link up with the airborne troops everyone hoped were already fighting inland.

Left: A member of the 8th Infantry Regiment shouldering a Browning machine gun and ammunition belt moves inland through a French village. After successfully landing on D-Day, the task of the forces from *Utah* would be to secure the flank on the beachhead and then start to move north towards the vital strategic port of Cherbourg.

Right: a view down *Utah* beach taken five days after D-Day. It was in many ways a perfect landing area, the broad tidal beach giving way to low dunes. The only drawback was the large area of impassable marshland behind the dunes. The only four roads across this had to be seized in the early hours of D-Day by the airborne for the invasion here to have any chance of success.

Below: Of all the German defensive measures along the Normandy beaches perhaps one of the oddest – and least successful – was the Goliath. These wire-controlled minitanks held a 83kg (182lb) explosive charge and were meant to come out of the dunes at attackers at anything up to ten miles (16km) an hour. On D-Day all of them were disabled or malfunctioned. These members of a US Navy Beach battalion examine those found behind *Utah.*

Below right: Airborne reinforcements fly in over *Utah.* Throughout the day three airborne landings of over 300 gliders brought in more troops inland to the beaches.

Above: US Army Engineers fix communication lines along one of the main streets of Ste. Mère-Eglise. Located at an important crossroads, this was an objective of the 82nd Airborne and was the first village liberated on D-Day.

Right: A member of the 82nd Airborne carries the belongings of a French refugee out of a Normandy village. For the thousands of French civilians in the invasion area, D-Day brought both the horrors of war and the hope of liberation after four years of German occupation.

Left: Soldiers of the 101st Airborne drive past an abandoned glider. By the close of D-Day, the 101st had secured its objectives – the beach exits – but had suffered 1,300 casualties and still had two thirds of its strength scattered and unaccounted for. The 82nd Airborne had taken 1,200 D-Day casualties and by the end of the day less than 40 per cent of its men were accounted for. However, it had secured a number of important crossroads and the outer perimeter of the *Utah* area.

Below: American airborne troops make their way carefully around a Norman churchyard. By the close of D-Day, contact had been made between the 101st Airborne and the 4th Infantry Division which had pushed four miles (6.4km) inland from the beach. Contact with the 82nd would take place the following day. In total, the 4th Division had landed over 21,000 men and 1,700 vehicles for the cost of 20 dead and 200 wounded. The beachhead at *Utah*, though still open to German counter attack, had been secured.

Chapter 4

OMAHA BEACH

Omaha was the second and last assault area of the American sector, which stretched in total for 37 miles (59km). Its assault beaches were 12 miles (20km) east of those on *Utah*. The first troops on *Omaha* were men from the 116th Infantry Regiment, US 29th Infantry Division and the 16th Infantry Regiment, US 1st Infantry Division, supported by men of the 2nd and 5th Ranger Battalions. *Omaha* was the objective of the US V Corps commanded by Major General Leonard T. Gerow, and was the second assault corps of Bradley's US 1st Army. Their time for landing was 06:30.

Right: In heavy swell and under grey skies, men of the US Coast Guard prepare to take their landing craft into the assault zone. In contrast to *Utah*, *Omaha* was to prove a costly beach to capture.

Above: Photographed from the battleship USS *Arkansas*, a ferry full of combat engineers makes its way towards the beach. Minesweepers of the *Omaha* Task Force had arrived offshore at 00:55, the first transports had arrived at 03:00. Like the procedure at *Utah*, the troops for *Omaha* were sent off in their landing craft 11 miles (17km) from the beach.

Right: The decision to send in the assault troops from so far out began to create confusion before the landing even took place. The first landing craft began making their way toward the beach at 04:30 2½ hours before sunrise and 2 hours before their time to land. In strong currents and in a 16-knot westerly wind, the flat-bottomed assault craft began to drift out of position and some began to sink. Here a US Coast Guard launch rescues a sailor from the water.

Top right: The naval bombardment which was meant to destroy the heavy German guns around *Omaha* began only 40 minutes before the landings. This was to prove inadequate for the task. After recovering from their initial shock and surprise, the surviving German coastal batteries began to fire back causing casualties such as the dead and wounded crewmen of this LCI.

Bottom right: With the assault troops out of position, and the German defences still intact, serious difficulties could be forseen when the troops finally landed. However, the ground over which the Americans would have to advance made the attack even more dangerous.

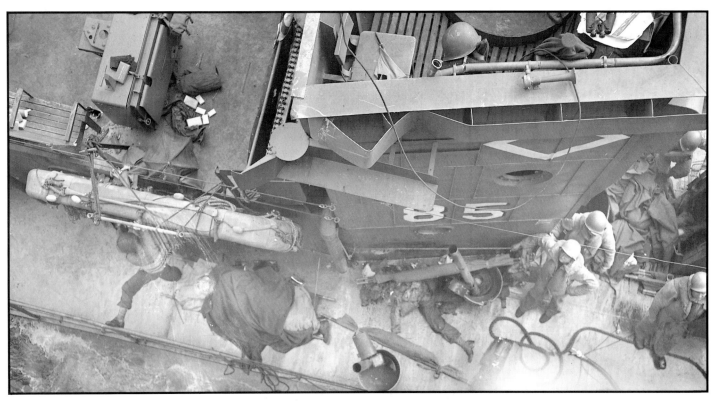

Above, below right, below left: Unlike *Utah*, the defences of *Omaha* were formidable, as can be seen from these photographs taken shortly after D-Day. Immediately behind the beach were high bluffs over 100 feet (30m) high, covered in trenches and bunkers and manned by the experienced German 352nd Division. There were only five exits through these bluffs, all of which were heavily defended. To get on and off the beach, the Americans had been trained in a specific landing plan. With units already disorganized at sea and suffering further disruption through beach obstacles and enemy fire, the landing plan collapsed and the assault began to dissolve into chaos as unit after unit became pinned down at the base of the high ground behind a low sea wall.

Left: While the struggle for the beachhead was going on, four miles (6km) to the west at a high cliff promontory known as the Pointe du Hoc, these men of the 2nd Ranger Battalion were taking part in one of the great heroic missions of D-Day. Given the task of destroying the casemated guns believed to be on the Pointe, the battalion scaled 100 foot (30m) cliffs to attack the battery from the seaward side. Bitter fighting cleared the casemates of Germans, but the Rangers discovered that the guns themselves had not been installed. Now in an exposed position and surrounded by Germans, the Rangers were forced to withstand a two-day siege before being relieved by forces from the beachhead.

Above left, above and right: By 08:00, with the tide rising four feet (1.2m) an hour and men and equipment crammed on the beaches and under heavy fire, it looked as if *Omaha* might have to be abandoned; but inspired by the leadership of officers such as General Cota of the 29th Division and the fighting qualities of the 5th Rangers, small groups of men fought their way up the bluffs and by 12:00 had broken the Germans' first line of defence. Aided by naval gunfire the advance continued, until by nightfall V Corps were 1½ miles (2.4km) inland.

Left: The bravery of the men on *Omaha* saved what could easily have been a disaster. But there was a heavy price to be paid. Their casualties on D-Day were 2,400 killed, wounded and missing. These French civilians tend the graves of one of the American cemeteries behind the *Omaha* beachhead.

Chapter 5

GOLD
BEACH

Gold was the first assault area in the British sector, its assault sectors positioned 15 miles (24km) east of *Omaha*. The first units ashore would be the 231st Brigade of the 50th (Northumbrian) Division and No.47 Royal Marine Commando. *Gold* was the objective of the British XXX Corps commanded by Lieutenant General G.C. Bucknall, one of the two assault corps of Lieutenant General Miles Dempsey's British 2nd Army. Their time for landing was 07:25.

Right: The Royal Navy cruiser HMS *Ajax* bombards German defensive positions in the *Gold* beach area. The naval bombardment of *Gold* began at 05:45 and lasted over 1½ hours. The *Ajax* was one of 95 Allied warships involved in the naval bombardment on D-Day.

Right: An Allied air reconnaissance photograph of German beach defences around the *Gold* area. Notice the soldiers running for cover on the left. This defensive layout was typical of the obstacles emplaced along the French coast. Every assault force on D-Day had to clear a way through such defences before getting ashore; a task made no easier by the millions of mines that had also been sown (below right).

Below: British troops ashore on *Gold.* Though held up by defensive obstacles, the landings went in on time. The objectives of *Gold* were the capture of the nearby town of Bayeux and the important Caen-Bayeux road, make contact with the Americans from *Omaha* and the capture of the seaside town of Arromanches – an important objective, as the town was to be the destination of one of the *Mulberry* harbours. (See page 10.)

Right: *Gold* beach after the first assault. Notice the stranded tank on the far right. This is one of the DD (Duplex Drive) amphibious tanks that were designed to spearhead the beach assaults on all D-Day beaches. Unfortunately the tank's canvas skirt which was meant to hold out the water often proved inadequate to the rough seas on the day and many tanks sank miles from shore. To prevent this, many landing craft commanders bravely delivered their DD tanks directly on to the beaches.

Below: The town of Arromanches, five miles (8km) west of *Gold*'s assault sectors and D-Day objective of the 231st Brigade. Six miles (9.6km) further along the coast to the west lay the village of Port-en-Bessin, where 47 Royal Marine Commando were meant to link up with the Americans.

Left: The commander of the *Gold* forces, Lieutenant General G.C. Bucknall, seen here with one of his senior staff officers Brigadier Pyman. *Gold* saw one of the most successful assaults of D-Day. By nightfall XXX Corps had cleared a lodgment area of five square miles (13km²), and forward patrols were within a mile (1.6km) of Bayeux. Arromanches had been liberated, and another three brigades were ashore and in position to advance; while further to the east, contact had been made with Canadian units advancing from *Juno* beach (see Chapter 6). In total, nearly 25,000 men had been landed for a cost of roughly 1,000 casualties. A real concern for General Bucknall, however, was that the commandos were still outside Port-en-Bessin and no contact had been made with the Americans. No one on *Gold* was yet aware of the terrible battle that had taken place on *Omaha*.

The Allies knew that the success of the D-Day invasion depended on the speed with which reinforcements could be brought ashore and a lodgment area secured. The task of preventing the Germans from reinforcing faster than the Allies fell to the aircraft of the Allied Expeditionary Air Force (AEAF), which consisted of the British 2nd Tactical Air Force and the US 9th Air Force, under the overall command of Air Chief Marshal Sir Trafford Leigh-Mallory, RAF.

Right: German tanks in transit by rail. The French railway system would be a prime target for the AEAF, as this was the method by which the Germans would have to bring most of their armour to the front.

Below: To stop them, an operation known as the Transportation Plan was put into effect. From early 1944, over 72 rail targets in France, Belgium and Germany were singled out for air attack, including bridges, junctions, marshalling yards and of course, rolling stock.

Left: Of 2,000 locomotives available in Northern France and Belgium, on D-Day only 500 were still operational. Elsewhere other air attacks were being made on radar sights, gun emplacements and airfields. In total over 14,000 individual sorties were flown on D-Day including vital anti-submarine patrols in the English Channel. The Luftwaffe could manage only 500 sorties in response.

Below: A US fighter is hastily rearmed by its ground crew. The AEAF swamped the German Luftwaffe by sheer numbers. On June 6, the Allies had available for action some 3,700 fighters and fighter-bombers and over 4,300 bombers of all sizes. To counter that force, the Luftwaffe in France, Belgium and Holland could only raise about 500 aircraft of all types. Allied air superiority was absolute.

Chapter 5

JUNO BEACH

Juno was the second landing area of the British sector; its assault beaches were a little over a mile (1.6km) east of those on *Gold*. *Juno* was to be the Canadian's beach, the first troops ashore being men of the 7th and 8th Canadian Brigades of the Canadian 3rd Division. *Juno* was the objective of the British I Corps commanded by Lieutenant General J. T. Crocker, the second assault corps of Dempsey's British 2nd Army. The landing was scheduled for 07:35, but was delayed to 07:45 for the 7th Canadian Brigade, and 07:55 for the 8th Canadian Brigade; making the 8th the last of the first wave units to land on D-Day.

Right: Weighed down with packs and struggling in the tide, these troops are seen coming ashore at Bernières-sur-Mer, *Juno* beach, some time after the initial assault. Notice that they also have to cope with bicycles – items of equipment very rarely seen in photographs taken after D-Day. The heavy damage sustained by the seafront buildings during the initial naval bombardment is also much in evidence.

Above: General R.F.L. Keller, commander of the Canadian 3rd Division, in conference with his staff on the *Juno* beachhead. The division's objectives were to move south to cut the Caen–Bayeux road and attack the Carpiquet aerodrome west of the city of Caen. It was also to link up with the British units coming east from *Gold* and west from *Sword*. (See Chapter 7.)

Right: One of the units which was to fight towards *Sword* was No. 48 Royal Marine Commando; members of No. 48 are seen here landing from LCIs. Because of the later landing times on *Juno*, the rising tide and heavy seas covered many of the German beach obstacles which took a heavy toll of landing craft on this particular beach. Nearly 30 per cent of craft coming ashore on *Juno* were damaged or destroyed.

Below: The landing of the French Canadian Régiment de la Chaudière. Despite the difficult sea conditions and German gun and mortar fire, the Canadians kept up their momentum, and by 08:15 the last units of the first wave were ashore and were making their way inland, bypassing those defensive strongpoints that could not be reduced immediately. By mid-afternoon the whole of the Canadian 3rd Division had landed.

Left: Sherman tanks of the Canadian 2nd Armoured Brigade land to give support to the infantry. By the close of the day, the brigade's armour would be on the Caen–Bayeux road, achieving one of its D-Day objectives by denying the Germans this important east-west axis.

Below: One of the first groups of German prisoners await transport back to England. Allied troops were surprised to find that many of the 'German' defenders on D-Day were in fact East Europeans and Soviets in German uniform. In all, the German Army had 13 battalions of such men in the region.

Left: Members of a Royal Navy Beach Commando on *Juno*. These men, like the members of the US Navy battalion on page 28 were the specialists in Combined Operations – the official term for amphibious warfare. Their task was to deal with problems on the landing beaches, allowing the ground troops to get on with the fighting inland.

Below: Troops of the 8th Canadian Brigade take cover from sniper fire amongst the wreckage of buildings and tank traps. Despite delays caused by actions such as this, by the end of the day the Canadians had in some places advanced up to seven miles (11km) inland, some of the greatest gains made by any units on June 6. Contact had been made with the forces coming in from *Gold*, but a serious gap of two miles (3km) still divided the Canadians from the units coming in from *Sword*. In all, 21,500 men had been landed on D-Day for the loss of nearly 1,000 men.

Chapter 7

SWORD BEACH

Sword was the third and last assault area in the British sector and formed the left flank of the invasion area. The British sector stretched for 24 miles (38km) bringing the entire *Overlord/Neptune* invasion front, together with the American sector, to 61 miles (98km) of Normandy coastline.

Sword's assault beaches were three miles (5km) east of *Juno* and were the target of the 8th Brigade of the British 3rd Division and Commandos of the 1st Special Service Brigade. *Sword* was the second objective of Crocker's I Corps. The time for landing was 07:25.

Right: The big 15-inch guns of the Royal Navy battleship HMS *Warspite* fire on German positions around *Sword*. The *Warspite* was one of the targets of the only German naval attack on D-Day. At 04:30 three German torpedo boats came out of Le Havre and attacked the fleet, sinking the Norwegian destroyer *Svenner* before beating a hasty retreat.

Above: Aircraft towing gliders full of airborne troops and equipment overfly the battleships HMS *Ramillies* and *Warspite* and the cruiser HMS *Frobisher*. All are bound for the *Sword* area.

Right: The view along *Sword* some days after the first assault. More heavily built-up than the other landing areas, *Sword* included the seaside town of Ouistreham, the D-Day objective of the first French forces to land – 176 French commandos led by Commandant Phillipe de Vaisseau Kieffer. The nature of the defences and German fire along the sea front led to a traffic jam of tanks and vehicles that did not begin to clear until 11:00.

Left: A Duplex Drive (DD) tank stuck on *Sword*. This photograph gives a very good view of the DD's collapsible canvas flotation screen.

Below: Past burning vehicles and through minefields and tank traps, troops make their way inland. *Sword* was one of the most important beaches in General Montgomery's strategic plan for the landings. It was only seven miles (11km) north of the city of Caen, a communications and transport centre that was vital to the German defence of Normandy. Caen was designated as one of the prime objectives of D-Day.

Right: The left flank of *Sword* and of the whole invasion front lay beyond two important waterways, the Caen Canal and Orne River. This is an aerial reconnaissance photograph of the bridge over the Caen Canal, known since D-Day as Pegasus Bridge, after the insignia of the British 6th Airborne Division. The land around this bridge and its neighbour across the Orne River was the first in France to be liberated. Its capture at 00:26 by an assault team of 181 glider-borne infantrymen was the first part of 6th Airborne's plan to secure a route through which the seaborne forces from *Sword* could advance.

Below: Under German mortar and machinegun fire these gliders sweep into land beyond the beachhead. These particular gliders were known as Hamilcars and typically would carry into battle a light Tetrarch tank. A regiment of these airborne tanks landed near the Orne River in the evening of D-Day in support of the 6th Airborne Division.

Above: German prisoners are guarded by commandos of the 1st Special Service Brigade. It was this unit which was the first from *Sword* to reach and cross the bridges over Caen Canal and Orne River.

Left: The airborne, being the first to fight on D-Day were also the first to risk death or capture. These men of the 6th Airborne are prisoners being filmed for German newsreels. It is estimated that of the 6,250 men landed by the 6th Airborne on D-Day, 650 were casualties by the end of the day.

Above left and above: The German defenders in Normandy were, for the most part, short of conventional artillery. As Allied troops began to fight inland from the beaches, they were mostly bombarded by mortar fire or subjected to barrages of rockets, which were given the nickname of "Moaning Minnies."

Left: A German Panzer V 'Panther' tank camouflaged against air attack. Together with the assault on *Omaha*, D-Day's other big crisis occured at about 19:00. From Caen, the German 21st Panzer Division launched an attack of 50 tanks into the gap between *Juno* and *Sword*. It was the only serious counter attack of the day, but it failed to reach the coast and was forced back to Caen by the weight of fire from ships, aircraft and ground troops.

Right and below right: Members of the 12th SS Panzer Division 'Hitler Jugend'. For the British and Canadians, most of the severest fighting to come in Normandy would be against SS troops such as these. The first units of the 12th SS Panzer reached Caen on the night of June 6 and were positioned to the west of the city around the Carpiquet aerodrome. The coming weeks would see bitter fighting between this division and the Canadians.

Left: Just a few of the 29,000 men who were successfully brought ashore on *Sword* by the end of D-Day. The situation by nightfall was mixed. The 3rd Division and the 6th Airborne had linked up and a German counter attack had been successfully repulsed. However, a large gap still existed between *Sword* and *Juno.* British forces were up to six miles (9.6km) inland, but Caen was still out of reach. Casualties were estimated to be about 1,000.

Below left and Right: Photographs which symbolize the success of the D-Day Combined Operations. DD tanks link up to support the airborne dug in beyond Pegasus Bridge.

Below: Royal Marine commandos dig in around a smashed glider. As night fell on June 6, Allied troops from all five invasion beaches dug in to await morning. The situation throughout the invasion area was fluid; the Allied front was not yet continuous or particularly secure, but nearly 133,000 men and thousands of tons of weapons, vehicles were ashore and more than capable of defending what had already been gained. The task would now be to expand and consolidate the bridgehead and to deliver more reinforcements before the Germans could build up a force to counter attack.

Above: The meaning of liberation. French children pose for Canadian war photographers.

As history was being written on the beaches of Normandy, the first the world knew of the D-Day landings was an official communiqué from SHAEF, broadcast in Britain by BBC radio at 09:33, June 6, a message also broadcast in the United States at 03:33 Eastern Standard Time. The simple statement, authorized by Eisenhower himself, read:
"Under the command of General Eisenhower, Allied naval forces, supported by strong air forces, began landing Allied armies this morning on the northern coast of France."

With those few words, notice was given that the final chapter of the war in Europe had begun.